# THE HUNT

# THE HUNT

## JASON DICKSON

BOOKTHUG : TORONTO MMVI

LIBRARY AND ARCHIVES CANADA

CATALOGUING IN PUBLICATION


Dickson, Jason, 1977-
The hunt / Jason Dickson.

Poems.
ISBN 0 9781587 0 9
I. Title.


PS8607.I34H85 2006     C811'.6     C2006-905524-6

*for Hugh Fulton*

All Aboard.

POST CARD

He wakes to the sound of water, and opening his eyes, to the belly of a ship. He looks upward to see his father look downward, who says, "Your mother has died." The son, who thinks he is dreaming, closes his eyes.

He sees his father later, building a fire, who noticing him says,

"Your mother is dead. She was killed by a man who is also a wolf. Do you understand?"

The son notices the other people on board, families, like his own, building fires. He hears the creaking of the boat, the sound of ice from outside entering the boards, the sound of someone moving, and knows that he is awake.

**ST. JOHN'S, Newfoundland**

Iceberg: Usually seen in coastal waters of New-
foundland every spring.

Photo by: Tooton's Studios

Pub. by Tooton's Ltd., St. John's, Newfoundland

*Post Card*

His sister is also on the
boat. She often sits with
her ear pressed up against
the hull. She hears the
sound of water through
the wood and objects that
hit the hull's side.

She says to her brother,
"Press your fingers into
your ears and you can
hear the same thing."

But her brother does like
most people on the boat:

sleep, cook, and sit with
their families. Some hide
behind boxes, or cry, while
others keep files, speak
quietly, or boil ice from the
boards.

He does not recognize any of
them, and does not look at
them, unless disturbed by
their yells, or startled by
their animals. As the ship
moves on, he sleeps less.

83865-C

**FERRYLAND**

(Twenty-five miles from St. John's)

Historic Ferryland on the Southern Shore is steeped in history and is a typical Newfoundland fishing settlement.

Photo by Tooton's Studios

POST CARD

USE CANADIAN POSTAGE

ADDRESS

Dist. by Tooton's Ltd., St. John's, Newfoundland

The boat enters a derelict fishing village in the middle of winter.

Several half complete structures still stand along the banks, and after the boat thaws and the snow disappears, the travellers rebuild the village.

Then take apart the ship and with the wood repair each building in order to restore the town.

S-1596

**HARBOUR MAIN, Newfoundland**
A fresh water creek draining into Conception Bay makes an ideal swimming pool for youngsters on a balmy summer afternoon.

Dist. by Tooton's Ltd., St. John's, Newfoundland

POST CARD

USE CANADIAN POSTAGE

ADDRESS

The son's project is to build a cart to ship wood from the boat to the buildings. He wears the serious face of his father, and though he's not able to build as well as his father, ~~he~~ assembles a likeness of the other carts. He finishes each edge, investigates the moving parts, and carves designs that he remembers from home onto the cart side.

The two children think about their mother, especially at night, when it is just a matter of days before they move into their new house. They sit on the beach watching their father finish his work. The sight of him moving down the new road with his lantern makes them proud. They watch him as they fall asleep.

S-1851

# TUCK'S POST CARD

CARTE POSTALE

(FOR ADDRESS ONLY)

DOWN NORTH ON THE LABRADOR. One of the sturdy fishing craft.

The daughter dreams about her mother. They are long dreams, with space, and strange sounds, where after waking the sky seems to fall to the beach like a body.

The son also dreams. His sleep is filled with long pauses where nothing happens, where he sits with nothing to do in a room or a house, the old house from before.

The father tells his children that they are not staying. They leave the cove a week later.

# TUCK'S POST CARD

CARTE  POSTALE

(FOR ADDRESS ONLY)

**A NORTHERN NEWFOUNDLAND VILLAGE.**
Cliffs rising abruptly from the sea are
typical of the North Newfoundland and
Labrador scenery.

As they move away
from the village, the son
builds walls ~~fine~~ with
branches along the edge
of the cart.

He is interested in their
shape, how each type

of bark feels different in
his hands. He builds a wall,
then a roof over-head. The
daughter, fascinated with his
project, gathers leaves to
fill in the holes. Soon a
canopy hides the two
children from the world.

WHARF FISHING VILLAGE, BAY OF FUNDY

address

Through the canopy the children watch small abandoned fishing ports pass along the coast. Sometimes a single house sits alone on a cliff, or a lighthouse appears, hardly standing. Shipwrecks rise on the shore and make a thick border along the water.

The daughter creates a game that separates sounds from the sound of waves, and for the next few days inside of the carriage the children take their time separating the sounds inside of the carriage from the sounds outside — sounds of birds, of the sea, and their father.

DISTRIBUTED BY SAINT JOHN NEWS CO., LTD.
SAINT JOHN, N.B.
PUB. BY THE BOOK ROOM LTD., HALIFAX, NOVA SCOTIA
PRINTED IN U.S.A.

**ST. JOHN'S, NEWFOUNDLAND**
**Quidi Vidi Battery Historic Site**
Reconstructed in 1967 to the original plans of 1830.
The battery overlooks the natural entrance to
Quidi Vidi Harbour one mile north of St. John's.

# POST CARD

POSTAGE
STAMP

ADDRESS

Dist. by Tooton's Ltd., St. John's, Newfoundland

In a village by the sea:

The father steps off his
horse and studies shop
signs. He is looking to buy
a map and a compass.

The son finds wood to fix
up the cart. He uses wood
from shipwrecks he saw
when entering town.

The daughter looks into
house windows. She looks
through curtains and tries
to make out people in the rooms.

Traveltime PRODUCT
S-2946

5

POST
CARD

ADDRESS

Dist. by Tooton's Ltd., St. John's, Newfoundland

The daughter is told to stay
and watch the cart, but
after her father and
brother leave, sounds in
the street draw her away.

She sees: a windchime
in a window, a lantern
in the window being lit
by a woman,

and hears: the windchime,
the voice of the woman
calling to someone in
the street.

The daughter wants to climb
up and introduce herself but
something holds her back. The
cart remains across the road,
blinking in between the
passing people.

The woman in the window
leaves and takes the lantern
with her. The light is gone
but she is still visible.

S-1856

**CORRESPONDENCE**

Meanwhile, up on the hill, a girl works in her gardens, unaware that the son is watching. He is uninhibited by the house that is near her, with its purple and restless interior. He feels invisible, from somewhere else. If she looks at me I will be transparent.

The sounds from near-by are of animals, birds and trees. He notices a small

**ADDRESS**

shed and moves toward it. Inside, he finds that it is full of tools. He stuffs as many tools as he can into his clothes and steals away along the trees.

In the trees sits the remains of a house and a half built ship. He is sick with their appearance. He looks up, frightened by the expanse of the sea below him, and the fishing boats that hover like small, purple stars.

The father purchases a map and attaches it to the carriage wall. It is two dimensional, sparsely illustrated with thick, dull lines.

And though the daughter doesn't understand it the first time, she understands it the second, her mouth

moving slowly as she words the towns and rivers that it places.

The name of their present town is a small dot on the farthest eastern shore. She looks left, across the body of land still to cross. Her mouth still, the space empty.

**CARTE POSTALE**
**POST CARD**

The carriage reaches the sea by the winter.

The colour of blue storms light up in the sky. Branches of ice collect on the carriage roof. The children hide in blankets. The father sits outside, in solitary conversation, and drives the carriage across the frozen water.

"We're going to Kanada, to Driersville, where the wolves live."

And later:

"Driersville. You never believe a word that I say."

**COURTYARD, PORT ROYAL HABITATION, NOVA SCOTIA**

This is a replica of the original Fort Royal Habitation which was built by Champlain in 1605. It is exact in size and detail and built on the original site. As in the original building, no spikes or nails were used. It is here that Champlain founded "The Order of Good Cheer."

*address*

They reach the main land and an occupied fort on its shore. The father climbs out into the square and removes the winter from his body like a coat.

He sits alone in the square, while his children sleep in the carriage, and watches the fort thaw - internally through its chimneys and stoves, and outside, from the springs that melt the ice.

The son wakes up believing that his arm is frozen to the floor. He is certain that if he moves it will break at the shoulder. He is afraid that the fort will freeze again, and that he'll remain alive, frozen in its stone buildings.

The ~~daughter~~ daughter rests. She digs a hole in the straw, sleeps like a fox, and shakes out the winter.

STRANDED VESSEL OFF YARMOUTH.

POST  CARD

The
C·W·F
Series

C. W. Faulkner & Co., Ltd., London, E.C. Series 694
British Production.

The son rebuilds the cart in the fort. He builds:

Thicker walls. Windows and doors. A stove. Shelves (stained red). An axle for the front.

He carves the shapes of buildings, people and shop names onto the exterior walls. He carves the shape of himself, the father, and his sister.

As they pull away and continue west the carriage develops a unique, interior sound. It pieces together a hum, a berth, its own space.

Cape Smokey, looking south along the Cabot
Trail, Cape Breton, N.S.

Published by John Urquhart Wholesale, Sydney, N.S.

U.S.A.

"Where is our mother?"
"She's in Driersville,
the Sunken Village."

And later:

"Where is Driersville?"
"I don't know. Look at
the map."

And later:

"Its not on there."
"We'll put it there, when
we find it."

C17890—Photo by Ray Martheleur

COLOR BY MIKE ROBERTS
BERKELEY, CALIF. 94710

The air is still when the children sleep. The floorboards collect scents from outside. They place the scents of lakes and fields.

On the floor of the room lays the dust, like the ground, that moves with the movement of the carriage. The scents of lakes and fields stir in the room, an atmosphere that, like roads, distribute space. Near the ceiling hang the sounds of voices and names. The names of the children are written onto the wood like constellations.

If the children would wake and not open their eyes they would feel momentarily abandoned, left outside, alone in an empty field.

Lighthouse at Peggy's Cove, Halifax County, Nova Scotia.    47

POST CARD

CARTE POSTALE

MADE IN CANADA

The sound of drums are heard through the carriage walls. When the children look through the window they see a house where lanterns move between rooms and the windows open and close like a pupil.

When the father pulls up to the house he is surrounded by a group of gypsies who introduce themselves and invite him to hunt. The father agrees and asks

that his son be included. The two grab their bows and leave the daughter behind to watch the carriage.

The gypsie children ask her to watch a play that is about to start in the basement of the house. She is led down into the cellar where the drums that she heard in the carriage grow louder.

BR-67

**CHURCH OF ST. CHARLES,** Grand Pre Park,
center of Acadian tradition.

An audience of children gather in front of a make-shift stage. The lid of a boiling pot is lifted and the water sends perfume into the room. Actors light lanterns in miniature houses and offer one to each child.

"This is the story of Drieksville, the Sunken Village. Of the wolves and ghosts who live there."

On the stage sits a miniature house and gypsie carriage. A candle is lit in each one.

We remember. There are beautiful buildings with antique gables and the streets are written like names on the ground.

PUB. BY THE BOOK ROOM LTD., HALIFAX, NOVA SCOTIA
PRINTED IN U.S.A.

MIRRO-KROME CARD BY H. S. CROCKER CO., INC., SAN FRANCISCO 1, CALIF.

address

place stamp here

Each home has been built up again and is concealed. To find them you have to be careful. You must avoid the common mistakes of passing through. If you are careful, the village will reveal itself, piece by piece, like a magic formula.

The candle is visible through the house and carriage wall.

Hide behind a house. In the middle of a room. All night, watching the village come.

Peggy's Cove
Nova Scotia, Canada

P54670

Plastichrome ® by COLOURPICTURE PUBLISHERS, INC. Made in Canada

Lewis & Nugent Ltd. (Wholesale Only) Halifax, N. S.

POST CARD

The daughter sits in the cellar corner and watches closely. Out in the field, her brother's hand catches in a metal trap.

A magician asks each child for a belonging. The son is carried back into the house by the father.

The magician makes two small figurines with the belongings.

They stand up when he places them on the table.

The son lies on a table one floor above. Pieces of metal are pulled from his fingers

The daughter forgets about her mother, her father, and her father's wolf. A clear glass is brought down over the figures and they still move.

Color Photo Courtesy Canadian Pacific Railway

ARTURA ARTURA
PLACE
STAMP
HERE
ARTURA ARTURA

Llonville Belgia

FOR MESSAGE

The daughter wanders upstairs, apart from herself, perceiving the smaller details of the house.

She watches people enter and exit rooms, people lean up against walls and people fall asleep.

FOR ADDRESS ONLY

She studies the currents of air in the halls, the shape of a door frame, and the sounds of a trap being cleaned in another room. She feels sleep working inside of her while she is still awake.

At dawn, she finds a sleeping body lying in a corner. The body is her brother.

*Kings Landing Historical Settlement, N. B., Canada*

**KINGS LANDING HISTORICAL SETTLEMENT**
New Brunswick, Canada
Wood for the open hearth cooking fire at the 1840
Ingraham House. Note the protective woolen apron.

So... so there are mountains
in the west?

Yes. Most are large, but there
are some this small.

And this map, it is...

Made with bark. The paints
are berries.

(pause).

Now what?

Oak.

photo: Marty Sheffer

Lewis & Nugent Ltd. (Wholesale only) Moncton, N. B.

ADDRESS

(pause).

Now what?

Water.
Dew.
Snow.
Wolf.
Rust.
Stone.
Lemon.
Gravel.
Fish.
Maple.
Cattle.
Moss.

Plastichrome
© COLOURPICTURE
Made in Canada

P307146

If I could, I would set traps across the entire country. I'd break myself into many men and hide near each one. I'd form a net of snares and pits and sit alone, waiting for the wolf to confront me. The land is full of bait that I set on the ground like a set of roads.

The camps he builds grow wilder. My father builds skinning racks that surround us while we eat. The fire light roams across them like a quiet storm, heating up in the wood and the bones.

Post Card

They terrify me. I shift in my seat all night, feeling my skin on me like a coat.

Birds avoid us. I take in the shapes of their bodies and incorporate them into my designs. I build racks spaced like the villages I see on the map.

The trees move less each day until I wonder if every animal has been killed.

I've never told them this, for I hardly believe it myself, but one day something extraordinary happened in an abandoned town that I scouted.

Most of the day was spent following a set of wolf tracks that led to the main road of a town. I knelt down to wait for the wolf and moments later, felt the presence of an animal, heard the sound of breathing in the street, although no wolf appeared.

Within moments, I heard the sounds approach although I faced nothing.

I was frozen, staring blankly ahead, until the sounds disappeared. It wasn't until a bird flew up from a roof that I moved and hit it dead-centre with my arrow.

It was the first night that I fell asleep before them.

Now I hide in my work.

K-133

Published by Thatcher Winger Associates Ltd., Utterson, Ontario

Made in U.S.A.

We only meet in an occas-
ional glance, a toss of food
from my hand to theirs,
or a startled look when I
notice something that is
behind them.

The nights begin to get cold
as the sounds of the forest
grow back, and I stare
at him when he isn't
looking.

I have a brother who lays
alone in the carriage; and
a father who always
returns covered in blood.

I find myself longing to know
more than I do, about my
sister, who collects cuts

POST CARD

like fruit, and about my
father, & whom I know
nothing.

I think of salves and med-
icine, & how the water is
never bare of insects, of
how the food is never
cooked. I think of fences,
& how there doesn't seem to
be any around, & how I'd
like to be inside one, like
a tree, looking out.

38139

Alma Street, Moncton, N.B.

The body of my brother, who loses his hand and has it replaced with a gypsy bandage, who has a fever and must stay in the carriage while our father drives, who wakes up with liquids in his mouth, like his chest is filled with syrup, like his mouth is made of wet grass, who is always heavy and cold.

I listen to the sounds of him. He is sick and a storm in the carriage. The purple lamp turns blue, and there is repair in his arms and in his bones, so I watch him carefully, and move with a low sound.

COPYRIGHT CANADA J.R. 1914

BOLTON PASS NEAR KNOWLTON P.Q.

# POST CARD

"VICTOR"          POSTAL.

The father is unable to find a road to the trade routes. Lost and without help, he sinks into the dwindling pace of the carriage, the limits of his thoughts, and the sounds that he discovers in the corners of his body.

He makes small noises as he drives

the carriage. Their volume grows despite his attempts to contain them. He develops an uncontrollable shudder in the lower part of his neck. He breaks into a rash and talks involuntarily.

He thinks about his wife and imagines her body still intact in the body of the wolf. He imagines how she will reach out to him when he opens up its stomach.

Près Ste. Marthe de Gaspé, P.Q.—Gaspé Highway at Ste. Marthe de Gaspé, P.Q.—SMG 4.

POST CARD

CARTE | POSTALE

THE PHOTOGELATINE ENGRAVING CO., LTD. TORONTO.

MADE IN CANADA

The daughter leaves the carriage at night to search the ponds that she finds in the trees. Tiny shapes appear in the water when held up to the lamp.

At dusk, the colour inside of their carriage is sometimes the same as the colour outside. The light is like a pond held in the air. The pots collect the light, and the illustrated mirrors fog.

SPINNING WHEEL. WAYSIDE SHRINE—C.F.R. Photos.
OUTDOOR BAKE OVEN, PROVINCE OF QUEBEC, CANADA

# POST CARD

483

## CORRESPONDENCE

The daughter is fascinated with the kettle. Its water turns to steam and rises into the air.

She stares into the kettle, lost in her thoughts, as the water boils. The son catches her sneaking back into the carriage with an empty kettle under one arm.

## ADDRESS

He asks where she has been, and she replies,

"At a pond gathering water. I filled a house up with steam to see what would happen."

"And what happened? he asks?

"It went quiet."

Corpus Christi Procession, Quebec.

# PRIVATE POST CARD

Printed in Belgium

1 c.
Canada &
United States
2 c.
Foreign.

This Space may be used for Correspondence.

This Space for Address only.

Cracks in the carriage accept the wind and make music between the boards. The children are hypnotized, turning around to face the sounds whenever a pitch or rhythm changes. The son listens closely to the sounds and sometimes calls out to them as if moved by a similar aeolian impulse.

The daughter lists words that correspond to each note and sound. It is a language that she hums to herself while working on the carriage.

Their carriage can be heard coming through the forest, as if a church were approaching, or a northern nocturnal orchestra.

A CALECHE, QUEBEC.

# PRIVATE POST CARD.

When the father comes upon the wolf, a complete and certain hunger is released. Its jaw becomes his fists, moving upward and apart like opening fingers. Its chest turns into a widening mouth, setting loose the throat and voice like a tongue. He draws apart the stomach where his wife sleeps, the place where she lays. He reaches into it.

In the end, he is covered with his wolf, their bodies scattered across the stable floor where the dogs and horses hide from him, turning their heads.

H. 204    W. G. MACFARLANE, PUBLISHER, TORONTO AND BUFFALO.

LA CALÈCHE DE QUÉBEC.    THE QUEBEC CALECHE, QUEBEC, CANADA.

# CARTE POSTALE

## CORRESPONDANCE

LIBRAIRIE — LG — GARNEAU L??
QUÉBEC

# POST CARD

## ADRESSE

417

A very old style of carriage, in use under the French Regime and preserved rather as a curiosity.

Voiture très ancienne en usage sous le régime français et qui a été conservée plutôt comme objet de curiosité.

An innkeeper comes out from his cellar after hearing some. one call from the road and finds the father inside of the stable with a wolf lying dead beside him.

.The father knows that it is the wolf he's been looking for. He knows C.L.C.

from the tracks that he followed into town, and from the town's deserted streets and houses. It was in the signs of secret habitation. The pale, blue windows of the houses, and signs that people were inside hiding in the basement. It was in the dog that howled on the edge of town, in the starving owls, and in the empty windmill.

The innkeeper understands the mistake. He explains to the father that the wolf is not from somewhere else, but that it is a wolf that has hunted in his village for years.

The villagers leave their cellars and gather the wolf's body into a grave. The church windows are blue with light.

The children are unlocked from their carriage and are invited to stay by the innkeeper, but the father refuses. He motions them back into the carriage and leaves.

The son props himself up to look out of the window as they drive away. He has a clear view of people looking at him through the windows of the church.

He imagines them under their house beds hiding from the wolf, their skeletons like his hidden in their bodies.

Wolfe Street Bridge, Sherbrooke, Que.

106.516.

At night the son talks in his
sleep.

Here is a village inhabited
by deer.
This is a place where someone
has left old machines.
Here is a cave with pictures,
like this one, and this one.
And this is a harbour.

You can see boats at the
bottom of the lake.
This is a place where the
wind plays music.
Here a river splits in two.
Here I saw a red bird, a
blue bird.
Here I found a half-buried
rabbit in the snow.
Here I saw a ghost.

MAIN STREET, DRYSDALE, ONTARIO.

# Post Card

The son sleepwalks
through abandoned
villages and houses.
He knows the
origin of each
house sound,
what specific
part causes it,
and what noise
will follow. When a
house sound stops
and re-arranges,
he moves asleep
between rooms, as
if he somehow

knows where to go.

Large, open squares. Windowed
rooms. Few places to go with-
out stepping into a white space.

I press against walls, secret
halls that contain old
children. I look out from these
houses like I look at the sky
from underwater. My body
is the sky. It is the sky. The
rain. The rain fallen.

Methodist Church,
Thorndale, Ont.

POST CARD

This Space may be used for Correspondence.

This Space for Address Only.

I wake to an empty
carriage. The sounds of
night fill my ears and
I look up to see my
brother wander into
the trees.

I follow him through
abandoned villages,
backyards, and crowded
rural cemetaries. He
stops and sits for hours
in an empty village
square.

Shapes appear in the
windows and in the
street. They are in houses,
a white        on the second
floor.

The lighting of a lamp. A
lit body. Our figures appear.

I sit with my brother all
night, watching the
village come.

POST CARD

For INLAND POSTAGE only this Space
may be used for Communications

THE ADDRESS ONLY TO BE
WRITTEN HERE

She sleeps two or three hours
a night and frequently wakes
to the smell of the open sacks
of bait kept on the shelf
beside her.

After the father hangs up his
weapons, and the son takes up
what tiny space he still inhabits,
the daughter has only a small
shelf on the corner on which
to sleep.

She wakes to the sight of her
brother leaning over her, half
visible under the green lamp,
before he disappears through
the wall.

I swear that my wrist broke
one evening, after waking and
screaming, though it
remained bent for days and
didn't hurt.

# POST CARD

For INLAND POSTAGE only this Space may be used for Communications

THE ADDRESS ONLY TO BE WRITTEN HERE

I wake up in the night choking, covered in water, rising with the memory of our old house.

I think of leaving, of vanishing like my brother.

When I wake to see him sleeping beside me, I wait, and press my finger to his face to see if he is still alive.

If I could change into some-thing else, like lightening or water, then I would remain.

I would be home, animate, falling into everything.

I am light, dull, illumin-ating white against the green wall.

# POST CARD.

G.

He mounts dead animals onto the carriage roof.

When the carriage is still, she senses the creatures above her looking out into the trees.

When the carriage moves their fastened feet hit the roof as is someone walked there.

I should mount one of my children to the roof. They are like rodents.

The blood of the mounted animals slips through the rotten ceiling onto the daughter while she sleeps.

I wake with red frost on my face, and the sounds of gunfire out of the window while I leap up to cry, and run out into the trees.

OLD ST. ANDREW'S CHURCH,
ST. ANDREWS, MANITOBA.

Old St. Andrew's Anglican Church on the Red
River was originally called the Rapids Church.
Built in 1849 it is the oldest church in con-
tinuous use in Canada, west of the Great Lakes.
It was here that Henry Budd, the first North
American Indian to enter the ministry, was
ordained.

I wake up and the
carriage door is locked.
There is a light in the
bushes, and for a
moment, I think my
father has returned.

A rifleman appears
and secures the back
door. He climbs up
into the seat and
drives the carriage
into the woods.

C21366 Color Photo by Ivan Lambert

Commercial Photo Service, Norwood 6, Manitoba

COLOR BY MIKE ROBERTS
BERKELEY, CALIF. 94710

U.S.A.

I call for my father through
the carriage window. I see
my brother disappear into
the trees. I think of setting
myself on fire.

The carriage stops. The rifle.
man climbs down and
vanishes. The forest is quiet.
The skin of my eyes pull
tight. My skin holds me in.
I lay myself carefully
down onto the floor.

POST CARD

ADDRESS ONLY

How much time has passed?
Light stays in the carriage
long after dark. Rust
climbs up the hitch like a
vine.

Scents collect like grass.
They grow in the wood.
The boards that shut me
in accept spectral
owls.

What are these teeth in my
mouth? This hair on the
back of my neck? The
bone in my hands?

How much time has passed?
Winter and spring appear
in the windows. The
cleaving fills with trees. And
the buildings rot, within a day.

## POST CARD

My mother was eaten by my father. She is inside of him. He is an eating wolf with my mother eaten alive inside of him.

My father and my mother swallowed me and brought me up. I know that and remember. I was brought up in a village and a house.

82477

If I lay each part that is my father down will she be what is left?

Your eyes are the eyes of your mother. Your teeth are her teeth. Wake up. Click them together. Light the lamp. What is that? Your arm, Laura. Laura. The room and the colour yellow.

The son's secret compartment
in the flow of the carriage:
compass, knife, paper, clock,
hatch.

in my hand: bone, blood,
muscle, pressure, pulse,
and space. Now (with
the knife) light

*Muriel Duncan*

*June 1941*

Portage La Prairie · "The Golden Heart of Manitoba" This Red River cart was part of the Prairie scene in Manitoba's history. A replica of this famous cart was built by base personnel at C.F.B. Southport and is on permanent display at the PORTAGE LA PRAIRIE CENTENNIAL MUSEUM. The Red River cart was driven from Jolliett, Quebec to Portage La Prairie, Manitoba during Manitoba's Centennial.

Maxwell Studios, Portage La Prairie, Man.

Prismatlex COLOR WILSON, DRYDEN, ONT.
Lithographed in Canada

14529R

## POST CARD

ADDRESS ONLY

I search for my brother in empty villages. In open squares, I look for his shape. Around me climb the shapes of houses. Their empty forms make music inside of them with the wind.

I love my brother and remember him. He is a shaped light inside of my brain. Inside of me he moves around and is remembered. My

brother: like a road in our village, like the sound of his name, like my mother only gone. If he was in a stomach, or a grave, then I would be able to find him. The carriage drives west, towards a clear-ing in the trees. Open and yellow light spreads out to me, like arms across the ground.

REAPING. INDIAN HEAD. ASSA. CANADIAN PACIFIC RAILWAY.

## CANADIAN SOUVENIR POST CARD

Ghosttown. People, houses,
three windows closing.
And closer, three houses,
one barn, five doors,
all closed.

There are people in the
houses. They illuminate
yellow against the blue
wall.

The people are birds. Their skin is open like a mouth, and I cannot help settling my arm inside. Air tightens.

Muscles stretch across me like a back.

POST CARD

CORRESPONDENCE HERE

NAME AND ADDRESS HERE

The inside of a bird has a
bottom like a lake. If you
look close enough, you can
see it move.

Clare Mich

R F D No. 2

You can pin a bird in
space and watch its insides
open like an opening fist.

Bertha

A Kipawa Moose,
on line of Canadian Pacific Railway.

1c.
CANADA AND
UNITED STATES.

2c
FOREIGN.

Made in Germany.

Published by Stedman Bros., Brantford, Canada.

352

THIS SPACE MAY BE USED FOR CORRESPONDENCE

THIS SPACE IS FOR ADDRESS ONLY.

Though like a lake, what contains a bird? What ability reveals itself at the bottom? What is buried? What will rise when I see it?

POST CARD

CORRESPONDENCE | NAME AND ADDRESS

PLACE POSTAGE STAMP HERE

I wake into the belly of a bird, with skin like branches, shaken, alive, taking place.

I wake upward where I open outward. My body unknown breaks into clouds.

When I disappear I will become
a bird. I will be air concealed
in feathers.

I am the inside of a bird.
Sparrow, come under my skin
and return to skin.

## Post Card

CORRESPONDENCE            ADDRESS

The bird mouth. My body lifts
off its tongue. Feathers light
yellow inside me.

Yellow feathers place the
windows of my carriage.
They articulate the interior.

A PROSPEROUS FARM HOME IN WESTERN CANADA.
Not many years ago this spot was unbroken prairie.

POSTAGE.

CORRESPONDENCE.

ADDRESS.

Ghosts appear at my camp-
site. They appear at the
edge of the fire and talk
to me. We are hypnotized
by the moving fire and
harps.

The ghosts tell stories of their
surroundings, how the fields
are made, how villages
begin. A wolf appears and
sits near me. It watches the
fire closely and it watches me.

ISSUED BY THE CANADIAN DEPARTMENT OF EMIGRATION,
1, REGENT STREET, LONDON, S.W. 1.

FORT MACLEOD, ALBERTA
Restoration of Sir F.W.G. Haultain's Law office on the
original site.

Pub. by John Patrick Photographers Ltd., Calgary

96258-C

post card

The Story of the Father and the Rifleman.

After abandoning both of his children in the forest, the father hunted wolves with the rifleman. He became the rifleman's apprentice in order to become a great hunter, in order to catch his wolf. He was told to sleep in the cellar of the rifleman's cabin and to be put under a trance. Only then could he become an obedient apprentice, and a great hunter of wolves.

The two men spent each day in search of game, the rifleman ahead carrying the rifle, and the father behind him, pulling supplies on a sled. The father learnt the rifleman's sport, and his shot became accurate. But under the weight of hypnosis, his body dulled. Each night, after the father was asleep, the rifleman entered and stored his catch, alive or dead, in the corners of the cellar. In his sleep, the father did not notice the shapes that enclosed him, the smell of blood, the decomposing remains.

*Heritage Park, "Where Happiness is History", Calgary, Canada*

The trapping of a real human being was the rifleman's final achievement in a lifetime of hunting. To his joy, the sleeping father in his cellar woke his cabin like a light. His happiness continued into most of the winter, until the darker days of February, when a disturbing notion entered his mind. Through one inexplicable event after another, the rifleman came to believe that his cabin was haunted.

Objects from outside began to collect in the corners of each room. Fur and pine needles fell from the rafters. Water gathered in little streams in the halls.

And indistinct animals passed through the walls of his rooms.

Night and day appeared. The seasons, weather, decay, entered and stayed. The changes were strange and irreversable. The house slowly opened.

The father found that at night, when he suddenly woke, the figure of a boy could be discerned from the dark. Barely visible, but still apparent, the boy appeared only for moments at a time, long enough to approach the bed, outstretch his hands, and reach for the father's throat.

Refusing to escape and leave his catch behind, the rifleman hid himself in the cellar with the father. He hid in a pile of carcus, living off of the raw meat, and waited. When he emerged weeks later, his cabin had vanished, and the father was nowhere to be found.

The only animal that remained was a wolf, half alive on the ground. The rifleman crept out of the pile of bodies to sneak away into the trees. When he was nearly out of sight, the wolf attacked, leaving him for dead on the forest floor.

786 Columbia Lake.

A wolf tells me about the body of my mother.

"What I understood about her, how she looked and how she felt. In the carriage you can see her everywhere."

The lamp turns orange.

The father and daughter stare into the fire.

"But what did I not understand?"

Pushing a stick in the fire, she says. Look. (pause) Look up.          A sky lit orange with embers.

787 Field - Golden Highway

The carriage is orange.
Its walls are an orange
light. The sound of air
settles. My son's body
arrives as a mist.

It becomes night. The
body of my daughter
is asleep on the floor.
The movement of my

eyes are red lights
moving in the room.

Towns on the plains
alight like tiny orange
ships. She says, the
carriage keeps me safe.
It holds my bones in.

All night, I watch my
family appear.

THE GREAT DIVIDE AT THE SUMMIT OF THE CANADIAN ROCKIES.

# POSTCARD

CORRESPONDENCE                                    ADDRESS

The foothills fall backward
into the dark. Their orange
light disappears. Father
I can barely see myself.
I can't tell if what is
there is still there.

The carriage fills with steam.
The foothills fill with smoke.

Father, for you, my voice,
and the name of our
mother calling us home.

Your son moves like
smoke through the
foothills.

*The Lakes in the Clouds*

J. Howard A. Chapman, Victoria, B. C. 1829

We are in the heart of the mountains. Father, tell me the story of Driersville, the Sunken Village. Of the wolves and ghosts that live there. Of my mother, held like a child in the inside of a wolf.

I can remember her beautiful face. I can see her looking out at me through the fur on your skin. Please, I will open you up and pull her out. Let me hold her when I sleep. Father, sleep and I will pass through you like smoke.

MTS. SHEOL & TEMPLE.  1309

J. Howard A. Chapman, Victoria, B. C. 1309

## Post Card

I pull my mother out from his stomach. I forgot how her arms reached for me and I am like a child. Her body is the red shape of a bird. I say her name, and open into the halls of our old home.

I remember. The halls opened into the rooms. There were rooms with tables and my voice

was written like a signature in the air. Each room was built up and it opened. I remember each piece and how it was.

Mother, I have filled up all of the glasses. The carriage is painted red. The lamps, lit outward, reach to him like arms and throats through the window.

722. NATURAL BRIDGE, FIELD. B.C.

It is evening in the heart
of the mountains. A storm
is outside. I enter villages,
in valleys. like mouths.
On the roads like throats,
I look for my brother.
I light red lamps and set
them against the purple
rock.

I draw the shape of my
family onto the ceiling.
"This is his name," I say.
Wait.        "This is the
sound of his name."

My brother is known, I
tell myself. No, I say,
he is not known.

Having his Picture taken at the Big Tree,
Stanley Park, Vancouver, B.C.

Barkerville, British Columbia: I build my brother out of empty houses. Furniture becomes his shape. He is the light of a lamp and the sound of a harp, hanging from the windows and doors.

A carriage is a musical instrument. It changes colour. Its temperature, sound and colour can be played. Walls and insides, but not always the same.

It is the music of colour, sound and space.

I find an observatory in the middle of a lake where, in the still wind, I see the stars beneath me.

The walls of my carriage become transluscent, like the thin membranes of muscle around my heart. Its skin plays a quiet song, and all is well.

POST CARD

CARTE POSTALE

Communication—Correspondance          Address—Adresse

Radium Mountains
    Radium B. C.

I build a grave in a
mountain pass.

Made of birds, for my
mother. Made of carriage
boards, for my brother.

I burn my father's body on a
pile of ~~bodies~~ birds and open
boards, and what is left
is left behind.

My face was red in his red
light.

COLOPHON

Manufactured in an edition of 500 copies in the fall of 2006 without assistance.

Originally displayed in the windows of One Dundas Street as part of the exhibit 'You Are Here' London, Ontario, Canada, June 18 - October 2, 2005 copyright © Jason Dickson, 2006

first edition

Printed in Canada

Designed by Jay MillAr

BookThug : 33 Webb Avenue Toronto Ontario Canada M6P 1M4

Distributed by Apollinaire's Bookshoppe : www.bookthug.ca